Anna Claybourne

www.raintreepublishers.co.uk
Visit our website to find out more information about **Raintree** books.

To order:
- ☎ Phone 44 (0) 1865 888112
- 🖹 Send a fax to 44 (0) 1865 314091
- 💻 Visit the Raintree bookshop at **www.raintreepublishers.co.uk** to browse our catalogue and order online.

First published in Great Britain by Raintree,
Halley Court, Jordan Hill, Oxford OX2 8EJ,
part of Harcourt Education.
Raintree is a registered trademark
of Harcourt Education Ltd.

© Harcourt Education Ltd 2006
First published in paperback in 2007.
The moral right of the proprietor has been asserted.

Editorial: Lucy Thunder and Harriet Milles
Design: Victoria Bevan and Kamae Design
Illustrations: Kamae Design
Picture Research: Melissa Allison
Production: Camilla Crask

Originated by Dot Gradations Ltd.
Printed and bound in Italy by Printer Trento srl

ISBN 1 844 21459 1 (hardback)
11 10 09 08 07
10 9 8 7 6 5 4 3 2 1

ISBN 1 844 43990 9 (paperback)
11 10 09 08 07
10 9 8 7 6 5 4 3 2 1

**British Library Cataloguing in
Publication Data**
Claybourne, Anna
Does a Worm Have a Girlfriend?: Reproduction
571.8
A full catalogue record for this book is available from
the British Library.

Acknowledgements
The publishers would like to thank the following
for permission to reproduce photographs:
Alamy pp. 28–29; Corbis pp. 12–13 (Frank Lane);
Corbis/Gallo Images pp. 7, 29 (mid); Getty
Images/PhotoDisc pp. 21–22; Getty/National
Geographic p. 8; Getty/Stone pp. 26–27; Nature
Photo Library pp. 16, 29 (bottom left) (Phil Savoie);
NHPA pp. 23 (George Bernard), 15, 29 (top) (M.I.
Walker); Oxford Scientific Films p. 25 (David M.
Dennis); Photolibrary.com p. 4 (Norbert Rosing);
Science Photo Library pp. 25 (Mark Burnett), 17 (Jack
K. Clark/Agstock), 18–19, 29 (bottom right) (Andrew
J. Martinez), 5 (Ed Young/Agstock), 11 (Paul Zahl)

Cover photograph of earthworm, reproduced with
permission of Ardea/Steve Hopkin.

The publishers would like to thank Nancy Harris and
Harold Pratt for their assistance in the preparation of
this book.

Contents

Some words are printed in bold, **like this**. You can find out what they mean on page 30. You can also look in the box at the bottom of the page where they first appear.

Lookalikes

Have you wondered why babies grow up to look like their parents?

Cheetahs have baby cheetahs. Dogs have puppies. Orange pips grow into orange trees. If a human has a baby, you can bet it will not be a cat, a frog, or a tomato. It will be another human. But why does this happen?

When cheetahs ▼ have babies, they always give birth to baby cheetahs.

No **species**, or type of creature can live forever. It has to keep making more of itself. Otherwise it cannot carry on existing in the world.

So, all living things **reproduce**. That means they have young, or **offspring**. The offspring are the same kind of living thing as themselves.

▲ *Oranges grow on orange trees. Inside each orange are pips (**seeds**) that can grow into new orange trees.*

offspring	young that living things make when they reproduce	**seed**	plant part that can grow into a new plant
reproduce	when a living thing makes copies of itself	**species**	name for a type of living thing

It takes two

Living things **reproduce** using tiny parts from their own bodies. These parts are called **cells**.

It usually takes two cells to have young, or reproduce. One comes from a female and is called an **egg cell**. One comes from a male and is called a **sperm cell**.

Most animals join together to make young animals. Sperm cells from the male join with egg cells from the female. The cells can then grow into eggs or **offspring**. They usually grow inside the female's body. Some animals, like swans, lay eggs. Others, like elephants, give birth to live young.

Using two cells to make offspring is called **sexual reproduction**.

Sexual reproduction

sperm cell

egg cell

fertilized egg

swan hatching

▼ Living things often form pairs. For example, male and female elephants join together in pairs to have baby elephants.

cell	tiny unit that living things are made up of
egg cell	female cell used to reproduce
sexual reproduction	when a male and female cell join together to reproduce
sperm cell	male cell used to reproduce

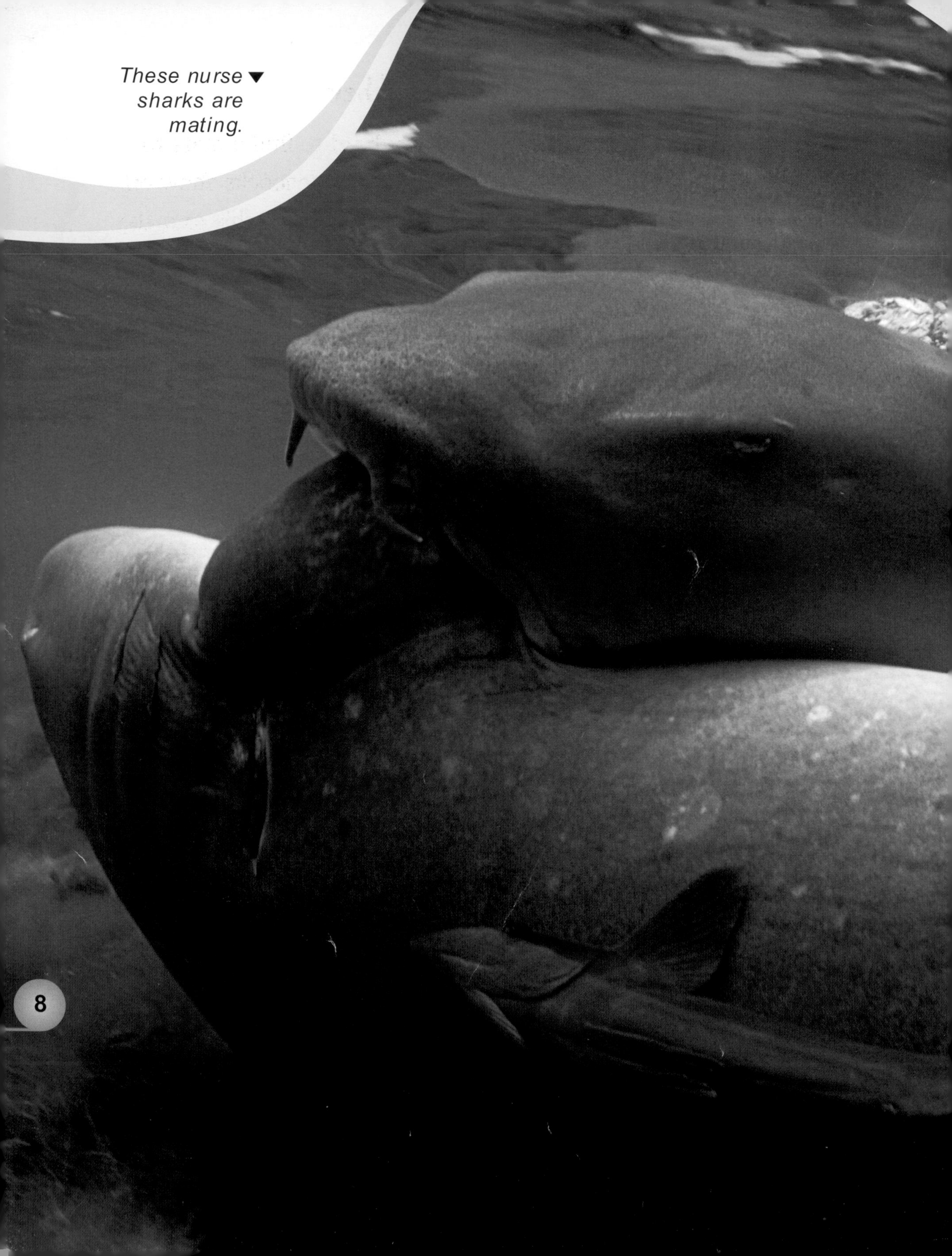

These nurse ▼ sharks are mating.

Getting together

Many animals try hard to find a mate to **reproduce** with. Male peacocks show off their bright feathers. They do this to make female peacocks see them. Other animals give off a scent to show they want a mate.

When a male shark finds a female, he chases her through the water. He tries to bite one of her fins. This tells her he is looking for a mate.

Then the sharks join together to have babies. This is called **mating**. The male inserts **sperm cells** into the female's body. The sperm join with her **egg cells**. The babies then start to grow.

A female animal is **pregnant** when she has babies growing inside her.

Shark fact

Baby sand tiger sharks eat each other while they are inside their mother's body. In the end, only one or two are left to be born.

mating	joining body cells together to make eggs or babies
pregnant	animal that has a baby or babies growing inside it

Pregnant dad

Can male creatures ever be **pregnant**? Believe it or not, they can!

In most **species**, only females have babies. But seahorses are different.

When seahorses join together to **reproduce**, the male has the baby. The female puts her **egg cells** into the male. They go in a special pouch on his stomach. There, the egg cells join with the male's **sperm cells**. They begin to grow into eggs.

After a while the eggs hatch. The male seahorse shoots the babies out of his pouch. They all swim away. There can be up to 300 baby seahorses.

Yes, this really is a ▶ pregnant male seahorse! The babies hatch out inside a pouch on his stomach.

Egg fact

300 baby seahorses might seem like a lot. But some animals have many more than that. The giant ocean sunfish can lay up to 300 million eggs at once!

Does a worm have a mate?

Kind of! Earthworms are different from elephants and sharks. Earthworms are both male and female at the same time!

Worms still get together to have babies. But each worm passes some male **sperm cells** to the other worm. Each worm joins the sperm cells with female **egg cells** in its own body. The egg cells of each worm are **fertilized**. This happens inside both worms. So both worms are **pregnant**!

Finally, both worms lay their eggs. These eggs hatch into baby worms.

fertilized   an egg cell gets fertilized when it joins with a sperm cell

▼ These earthworms are **mating**. They swap **cells** so that male and female cells can join together. Both worms will lay eggs and have babies.

Female ... or male?

The blackspot angelfish can start life as a female, and then turn into a male halfway through its life!

Doing the splits

Most living things use **sexual reproduction**. This is when female and male **cells** come together to form **offspring** (young). But there are some creatures that never need a **mate**. They can produce offspring on their own.

Think of an **amoeba**. It is a simple animal that has only one cell. Amoebas are tiny. They are too small to see, except through a **microscope**.

When an amoeba wants to **reproduce**, it just splits in two. Each part becomes a new amoeba. Each new amoeba can also split in two to make two more.

Amoebas reproduce on their own. They do not need a mate. This is called **asexual reproduction**.

This is a microscope picture ▶ of an amoeba. An amoeba can split into two. It can become two amoebas instead of one.

amoeba	simple animal with one body cell
asexual reproduction	offspring made by only one parent
microscope	machine that makes things look bigger

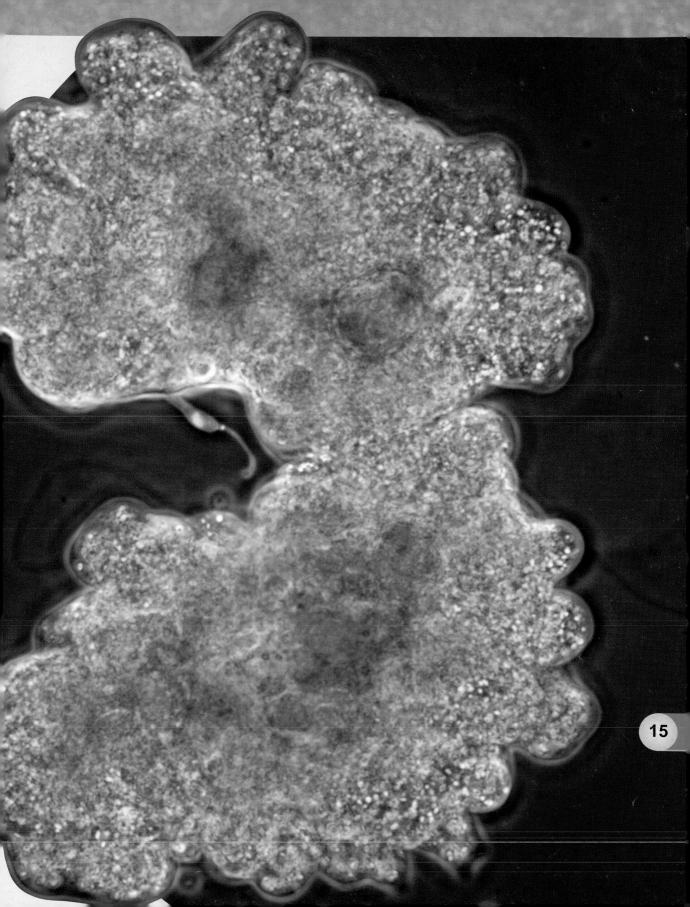

15

All desert ▼
grassland whiptail
lizards are females.

Lady lizards

Desert grassland whiptail lizards only come in one sex – female.

Each whiptail lizard lays eggs that hatch into more female whiptail lizards. This way of having **offspring** is called **parthenogenesis**. It is an unusual type of **asexual reproduction**, where only one parent is needed to make babies. No males are needed! This is just as well, since there are no males around.

So, why can't a whiptail just **mate** with a different kind of lizard to **reproduce**? The answer is that this would not work. **Mating** only works with a mate of the same **species**. There are no male whiptails, so the females never mate.

Aphid alert!

Some insects, such as aphids, use parthenogenesis too.

parthenogenesis having offspring by laying eggs without mating first

A baby from an arm

If one of a starfish's arms gets broken off, guess what happens! The arm grows a new body. It grows a mouth and four more arms to make a new starfish! Meanwhile, the first starfish will grow a new arm. They are both complete starfish. One starfish has become two.

This way of **reproducing** is called **regeneration**. It is a kind of **asexual reproduction**. This means there is only one parent.

Starfish can also use **sexual reproduction**. Males and females release their **cells** into the sea water. Some of the cells bump into each other. They join together and grow into baby starfish.

Worm fact!

Flatworms are a type of worm. They can regenerate too. You can cut a flatworm into ten pieces, and each one will grow into a new flatworm.

regeneration making offspring from a broken-off body part

▼ *This starfish is growing from an arm that has broken off another starfish.*

Flower power

Plants, such as poppies, **reproduce** when male and female plant **cells** come together. They make **seeds** that can grow into new plants.

But how do male and female plant cells come together? Plants are rooted in the soil. They cannot move around to look for a partner.

The answer is through **pollination**. Insects land on a poppy flower to feed. They pick up male plant cells called **pollen**. When the insects visit another poppy, they leave some pollen behind. There, the pollen cells join with female plant cells. The female plant cells become **fertilized** and grow into seeds. This is pollination.

Some plants use wind to help them reproduce. The wind carries the pollen cells. Then the cells land on other plants.

Pollen fact

*Pollen cells can only join with female cells from the same **species** (type) of plant. If pollen lands on the wrong type of flower, it will not reproduce.*

pollen	male plant cells that look like yellow dust
pollination	joining male pollen plant cells with female plant cells to make seeds

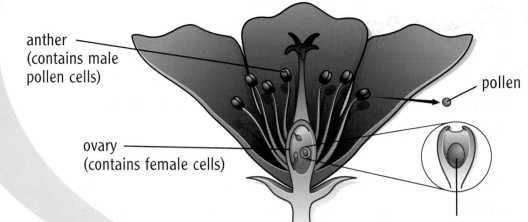

anther
(contains male
pollen cells)

pollen

ovary
(contains female cells)

female egg

Seed pod

Poppy flower

Plants use their ▲
flowers to reproduce.
After being fertilized, the
flower makes seeds.

Strawberry invasion!

If it was left alone, a strawberry plant could take over your whole garden!

Strawberry plants grow special branches, which become new plants. They are called **runners**. They creep over the soil. Then they take root, and become new strawberry plants. Finally, they separate from the parent plant.

In this way, one strawberry plant can make lots of new strawberry plants. The strawberry makes copies of itself without a **mate**. This is a type of **asexual reproduction**.

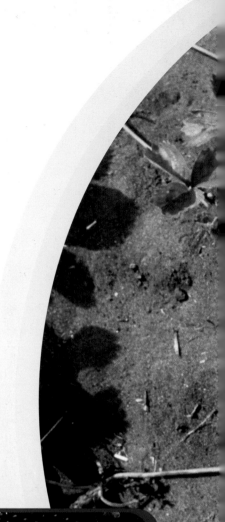

More strawberries!

*Strawberries can also use **sexual reproduction**. **Pollen cells** from strawberry flowers join with female strawberry cells. The female cells become **fertilized**. Then the **seeds** form. You can see tiny strawberry seeds all over a fresh strawberry.*

runner   shoot that can grow into a new plant

▼ This strawberry plant can spread out runners that turn into new plants. It can take over all the land it can reach.

Runner

Passing it on

Living things pass on their own special qualities to their **offspring**. This also happens in humans.

Try this. Check your earlobes in a mirror. Do they hang down? Do they run straight across to join your head? Whatever they look like has been decided by your **genes**.

Genes are the instructions inside the **cells** of living things. They tell all living things how to grow and work.

Genes explain why offspring turn out to look like their parents. The cells that make a baby contain copies of genes from both parents. So a baby gets a mixture of instructions. Some come from its father and some come from its mother.

Because of this, everyone is the same **species** as their parents. They will even look similar to their parents. But each person also has their own special pattern of genes.

genes instructions inside cells that make living things work

▼ If you have "hanging" earlobes, your earlobe hangs down below where it is attached.

◀ If you have "attached" earlobes, your earlobe runs straight across to join your head.

26

Your genes can make it ▲ possible for you to be naturally good at something. But you can still learn more, and get better!

Who am I?

So now you know how you ended up human. You had no choice! For thousands of years, humans have been having baby humans. They grew up to have more baby humans, and so on.

At the same time, **amoebas**, seahorses, sharks, lizards, and strawberries have been doing the same thing. They pass on their own **cells** and **genes**. They do this to make sure their own **species**, or type of living thing, keeps going through time.

Your surroundings and the things you do also help to make you the person you are. For example, eating healthy food makes you grow stronger. Practising makes you better at sport or playing an instrument. Studying helps you learn more.

So, you can make the most of whatever you are given!

Reproduction rundown

Type of reproduction

SEXUAL REPRODUCTION

Animal

A male and female **mate**. They join male **sperm cells** and female **eggs cells** together. This makes a baby, or an egg that can hatch into **offspring**.

Plant

A plant releases male **pollen** cells. Wind or insects carry the pollen to another plant. It joins with female **cells**. This makes **seeds** that can grow into new plants.

ASEXUAL REPRODUCTION

Splitting

One living thing splits into two to make two living things.

Regeneration

Part of a living thing breaks off and grows into a whole new living thing.

Parthenogenesis

A female lays eggs without mating or exchanging cells.

By runner

A plant puts out **runners** that can break off and grow into new plants.

How do they reproduce?

Can you remember which kind of reproduction these living things use to make their **offspring**?

A. Poppy

B. Amoeba

C. Elephant

D. Starfish

E. Desert grassland whiptail lizard

Answers

A. Sexual (plant)
B. Asexual (splitting)
C. Sexual (animal)
D. Sexual (animal) and asexual (regeneration)
E. Asexual (parthenogenesis)

Glossary

amoeba simple animal with one body cell. Amoebas are so small you need a microscope to see them.

asexual reproduction offspring made by only one parent. Amoebas reproduce this way. Strawberries can too.

cells tiny units that living things are made up of. Some creatures have billions of cells, while others have only one.

egg cell female cell used to reproduce. When animals mate, egg cells join with male sperm cells.

fertilized an egg cell gets fertilized when it joins with a sperm cell.

gene instruction inside cells that makes living things work. Your genes are passed on to you from your parents.

mate/mating joining body cells together to make eggs or babies. Most animals need to mate in order to reproduce.

microscope machine that makes things look bigger.

offspring young that living things make when they reproduce. For example, a tiger cub is a tiger's offspring.

parthenogenesis having offspring by laying eggs without mating first.

pollen male plant cells that look like yellow dust.

pollination joining male pollen plant cells with female plant cells to make seeds. Pollen gets carried between plants by insects or by the wind.

pregnant used to describe an animal that has a baby or babies growing inside it. Usually, only female animals get pregnant.

regeneration making offspring from a broken-off body part. Starfish and flatworms can reproduce this way.

reproduce when a living thing makes copies of itself. All living things reproduce in order to keep their species going.

runner shoot that can grow into a new plant. Strawberry plants have runners.

seed plant part that can grow into a new plant. You can find seeds in the middle of an apple.

sexual reproduction when a male and a female cell join together to reproduce. Most animals reproduce this way.

species name for a type of living thing. Creatures always have babies that belong to the same species as themselves.

sperm cell male cell used to reproduce. When animals mate, sperm cells can join with female egg cells.

Want to know more?

Books to read

- *The Usborne Book of Genes and DNA*, by Anna Claybourne (Usborne Publishing, 2003)
- *What Makes Me Me?*, by Robert Winston (Dorling Kindersley, 2004)

Places to visit

- Life Science Centre
  Times Square
  Newcastle upon Tyne
  NE1 4EP
  United Kingdom
  Tel: 0191 243 8210
  http://www.lifesciencecentre.org.uk/home.php

To find out more about different species of living things, have a look at ***Can You Tell a Skink from a Salamander?***

Did you know that different living things are specially suited to their surroundings? To find out how, read ***Would You Survive?***

Index